AF437101

Another Thing to Think About

By: Lance Carter

Dedicated to all the librarians.

Always busy, always moving around,
but hardly ever making
a sound.

Another Thing to Think About

Car Wash Poem #1

Lightning strikes like
modified wheels on a mountain bike,
and the wind wraps around
this upside down town
past a cold metal box
at the car wash.

People

People from the past fall into and become
people from the future
and it goes this way and I can hardly remember
where they are or where they've gone.
People now are fine,
people become representations of passing time,
but some nights I wonder why
they'll find
me in some late park,
or driving tiredly through the dark.
People change their ways and the days
spent with them become filled with a warm haze.
When spring hits,
a sharp, fresh wind
brings me out of my daze.

Eddie Sunwell

Eddie Sunwell spent the vast majority
of his days and nights
over a restaurant grill, surrounded by
coworkers he liked
while his wife and kids were home.
But some nights, after the lights
in the lobby had been turned off
Eddie could be heard reciting goodnights
over the phone.
And his voice blended perfectly
with the fryers' tone.
Miles away, his kids rested their heads
while his coworkers wished they were also in bed.

One Night

One night, under stars
and harsh gas station lights
I found my breath caught hanging in the air.
And beside me, a girl's breath and mine made a pair.
She told me she loved my friend,
I bought her a coffee
and then
she was running across the
street, and I never saw her again.
It was a night when
you could feel your bones
hit by the wind.
I had a long walk home
but I sat and thought of my friend
because it all seemed so important
but it wasn't,
or was it?
Before too long, even that night moved on
like the girl that was gone
and who left no trace,
save the absence of a smile, on one boy's face.
Well, neither one nor the other saw
themselves or each other
ever again.

Nighttime in the Suburbs

As the sun goes down behind the gate,
I hope that my friend won't be late.
And the moon is rising in the sky,
before long I'll be lost in the night.
I'm not sure that I'll make it back home.

My house looks like the one next door,
and my neighbors never come out on their porch.
I'd like to have them over and around,
but I never hear them even make a sound.

These quiet and thoughtful nights,
are sometimes the best thing in my life.
In the morning I'll get up and go work,
I'll see what's new down at the store.
At five I'll leave and come back home.

My neighbors and I have the same car,
and I never ever see them in their yard.
I'd like to let them come and watch TV,
but they're probably just tired like me.

Bicycles

I miss the time when I was younger.
Not the things that happened
when I was younger
but the time when I was younger.
You used to look past me
with eyes filled with hunger
with desire and with wonder
for what life would be like when
you and I were older
and in high school.
But right then we were on bicycles
and our smiles
and the sparkle in the air
traveled up and down the trail
with us for miles
and stayed with us as we tore
ceaselessly into our futures.

We arrive at the present only to realize
it has already past
so we're thrown back and forth like this
in a never-ending slide called time.

Boxes

In my head is cardboard boxes filled
with everything anyone who's ever talked to me
has said.
Every now and then I'll pull one out
and remember the sound, say,
my cousin made
when he smiled
while opening a present.

Sometimes one will fall off a shelf,
accidentally
so that I'm hit
suddenly
with a dusty memory.
Often though,
more often than not
I look to find that a box has been lost
so I hang on tight
to the ones that I've got.

The Life of Antoinette Pennington

Antoinette Pennington
with her eyes crossed
and her head full of thoughts
never stopped to look at the sky,
never stopped in the park to watch
the birds fly by.
She never quite saw the look
in her husband's eyes,
and never quite listened to
her friends when they cried.
Never saw her breath in the morning light,
never saw the sun dancing
through her blinds.
And most of us
never even
saw her
go by.

Another Thing to Think About

In a place I'm often found,
in a train car underground,
the train I'm in speeds on silver rims
inside, a boy leans in
and tells me of the life he's been living.

The boy is fifteen,
younger than me,
yet his eyes hold the wisdom of centuries.

"It seems to me" he whispers secretly
"that everything we've ever seen
has already been"

"If ya think about it,
it's all just waves"
a smile spreads on his face.

"The rising of the tides,
the day and night of the skies,
and the blinking of your eyes.
They're all repeating loops
that never seem to die"

My pulsing headache makes me close my eyes,
and the sun rises
and so do the tides.

A girl down from me gets off the train
and tomorrow she'll be back to get off the same way.

Colors,
lights,
sounds,
and ideas,
are all very real
and they never sit still.

All that I can see with my very own eyes
is all a beating heart for the galaxy's mind.

I Cleaned Up

I always cleaned the house
before she came.
In hopes that her
perception of me wouldn't be stained
like dried toothpaste around my sink drain.
If we stayed that way,
it would have remained
that I be expected to never change.
Thankfully, clean plates
is all that remains.
And me,
I changed…
like all things do.

Slowly

Slowly
people walk down a dimly lit hall,
and slowly
blood drips down past them all.
Slowly
people move so they don't get blood on their feet,
and just above them
a man dangles, and he
screams
and laughs
and spins and
cracks jokes,
but the people walk by, and don't know, so
he yells
and he cries
and eventually dies.
Then the people slowly tilt up their eyes.

September

The days of September,
just before the start of fall
seem to drag on the longest of all.
When even the birds in the sky
appear to fly by
like lines
on the side of the road.
I'm not sure where to go as I drive down a cardboard
street,
the people in the vehicle next to me
don't seem to be too sure either.
But by the time the sun slowly drops down,
I'll be back home to
look at the stars in the sky,
and they're brighter than the days that will come and
go by.
Everything's sleepy and winding down,
tomorrow time won't go by at all.
Then it'll quickly speed up,
and we'll be into the fall.

Future

The future
is about as familiar
as the ghost of a caterpillar,
and I'm not sure I care
about the things people say will
matter later.
The place I'd like to be
is a poem,
a film,
and a meal, every evening.
And then, after some late-night TV
I'll ask myself where I've been
and where, someday, will I be?
But I'm asking myself that now,
and I hope by the time I find out
I won't be lying back down
on the concrete
ground.

Untitled

He looks at her as if she's a painting,
and she recites words as if she's an actress,
trying to convince him that what she's saying is real,
all the while convincing herself.
And like a camera it goes right
through him, and he zooms out to
see someone several miles away
reciting the exact same lines.

Outside, his car engine ignites with the
thoughts of tomorrow.
She hopes he'll make it home okay.
He does too, because the clouds are hiding the moon.
Standing in the streetlight, he waits a
moment longer, not moving an inch,
in hopes of staying there forever.
But tonight is already over,
and tomorrow sleeps with him
through his dreams
and wakes with him in the morning.

Car Wash Poem #2

Night has fallen on Overland Park
and in the dark
the cars leave the wash
and retire home to watch
TV
and prepare for sleep.

We Used To

We used to dance in fields
on days when we'd only eat two meals
and wait till the stars came out to steal
kisses and share thoughts
under the blanket that was the photos we'd find
tomorrow.
We used to fight about who was right
and get so mad that we'd call it a night.
We used to watch the clock spin by
and sit on colorful rugs under fluorescent lights.
We always wanted
these moments to go by
But now we can't go back,
no matter how we try.
So the fields are empty, and the classrooms are too
and all the empty buildings remind me of you
and me
in some park
under some tree
or lost
in some distant memory.

The Life of Don Thompson

Henry Locke's one claim to fame
is being the one who shot the man
who could've became
the father to children
with a woman to whom
he'd recently become engaged.
But this man died months before
the bullet entered his brain.
Most likely around the time a letter came,
bearing his name: Don Thompson.

Don Thompson's one claim to fame
can be found written in a small
newspaper in Hays.
Written and told on merely half a page,
the story follows Don and his fishing days.
Don set and held the record for the largest
catfish ever caught in Hays.
It was obtained one hot day,
on a pond, in May.
The bread from Don's boat
attracted fish and in a craze
they would swim over and over each other,
slimy in the haze
of the sun.

Water splashed from their fins to the boat
as they each pushed and shoved
to try and get the most.
Deep in Don's chest,
a spark began to light
as he watched the fish
fight and fight and fight.
A hand touched his hand
and he was brought back to the light.
He smiled at the face of the girl that he loved
and for the rest of time
he was lost
in her eyes.
Even as he lied
on the battlefield dying,
there would be no fear
and there would be no crying.
For in the wavy light of the sun,
Don saw only one
thing,
and he began to fly.

Some fight for food, and some fight to survive,
in this case Don did neither, and he died.

Smile/Time

Her smile is time
and all the times spinning around
from fall
walks past even faced folks at the mall
hands brushing and fingers locking
under Christmas lights and walking
down streets and all around town
she sings *Lover, You Should've Come Over*
and I do
and I know that I love her
and she loves me too.

Searching

He's searching,
searching for something
the rest of us can't see.
He's gliding and tumbling
and flying around with his
arms stretched wide,
high above the ground.
He's looking for a thing
something profound,
and someday,
again,
his feet
will touch the ground.
But by then,
the rest of us won't
be around.
So with new knowledge gained
and the sun in his face,
he will fly out again
over an endless sea.

Chasing the Dream

The sun drops,
slowly,
like it does every evening,
as if someone is belaying it,
bringing it to safety.
In this hour, a boy meets his grandparents
in the parking lot of his work.
It is his birthday and they came to surprise him.
He spares one more glance, and
waves back at me, squinting through the
spotlight of the sun.
For a moment he wavers, drawn towards the light,
but something in his head pulls him away.
Arm in arm, he exits with his grandparents
as I, and another man, watch him go.
The man takes this moment to remove his cap
and run his fingers through his hair.
It feels good, and the sun is warm so he breathes in
the golden air.
Our eyes connect and he smiles at me, I nod
but his attention is drawn to the horizon.
I can almost see his daydream.

There's a highway that runs through our town,
I can hear the cars from my bedroom at nighttime.
In one direction, it goes straight to the city,
and I go there on Saturday nights.
In the other, it goes to the country,
and beyond that,
I don't know.
Someday, when I'm ready,
I'll get on the highway and chase the sun over rolling
fields.
Occasionally resting for the night,
or pausing to wait out the rain, but
never coming to a complete stop.
Until I reach a place
where the sun never sets.

Flowers

The pictures hang on the wall,
they remind me of last fall.
And the times we laid on the grass
watching the day go past.
The evening light slipped away
and the light dried off of your face,
until we were left with darkness.
Darkness and…

Your eyes blossomed
and your feet turned to grass
just another sign of the day going past.
Your cheeks to roses
and your smile to thyme,
somewhere in the distance a part of me died.

Heat

Liquid heat rises from the grill
and taints my windshield well
like mirrors in a clownhouse jail.
Everything is what it is in the sun
and the heat comes down and makes everything run.
Someday I'll get shot by a gun
from my upstairs neighbor's
second wife's mom.
For now, the heat makes everything spin
and a man three blocks from me, and I, share a grin
but it's all too still, so I sit and wait
for the wind.

There's Very Little I Have to Do
(Before I Realize That the World Will End Someday)

If you take a walk downstairs
and out into the backyard
you'll find under three layers
of rock,
a fleshy face
that talks.

When I've listened in the past,
its told me without being asked:
what will be the death of my best
friend and
how the world will end and
how under three layers of rock
the world is a lot darker
than you could ever imagine.

But if you cover him up and
go back inside,
you'll find that your house is
a warm safe place to hide.
By the time the evening light wipes
the food off your plate,
you'll realize that the face likely never
existed in the first place.

For Eyes

Maybe we never truly know ourselves,
the thought floats through my mind now
as I stare at the unwavering reflection of
myself in the paneless window.
What am I thinking?
I don't know.
But I like the way the collar of my shirt rests
like diamonds on my shoulders,
and I smile.
Who am I?
I have four eyes, twenty fingers, two mouths,
and an unblinking reflection that won't stop staring.
Haunting me through the night.

Untitled

I hate taking photos because
the camera doesn't see me
the way my eyes do.

But I love when she stares
at me because her eyes see me
the way mine don't.

The Life of Lisa Versche

Lisa Versche says humans weren't meant to
travel on planes and
40,000 feet up in the air
a woman is scared
and says something
that is recorded and played
back for the masses to decide if it's real.

Lisa Versche says through a beer
that she has better other things to worry about this
year,
like if her football team will win again
or when
the prices of car washes will go back down
but then
Lisa Versche has other problems too.
Things she's too afraid to say,
like how with every quickly passing day
her hairs turn gray and gray
and day by day
she's taken farther away from a time when time
moved
slowly.

Lisa hardly remembers nights as a kid and that makes
her who she is
but she remembers
raisins,
markers,
scooters,
and her best friends,
who have now been gone for a long time

and her kids who have moved on to the rest of their
lives.

Lisa from across the shopping mall is
someone who, you might say,
has it all.
So it's confusing,
you decide,
when Lisa yells at an employee
at the clothing store.
You remind yourself that luckily
someday she won't be around anymore.
And that's true.

Rainstorm

The sky makes a sound like bowling balls,
and the storm opens up its eye to watch through
a rain-soaked window as you sleep.

The storm is back,
just when you thought it had
forgotten about you.
Just when you had forgotten about it,
it came back,
like it always does,
creeping, slowly at first, and then fully present.

Like a toy that you thought you lost,
or an old friend you thought you forgot.
It came back to remind you that
some things never change.
The truth is, it never really went away,
just hid for a while, right out of sight.
It's been following you through your
rickety, unstable life, and now it's here to
help you through the night.

When you wake up, it will be
hiding
again.

One Poem for Her

Her scent fades until
all I can remember,
vaguely
is
her face and her name and
sometimes at night when I'm laying in bed,
I'll remember something that she said
or she did and
as the memory wanes
my consciousness fades.

But someday I'll see her in the
backseat of a truck on the highway
and wonder how we ever met
and why we don't anymore.

Round and Round

Sometimes I get dizzy,
and the room where I wake
and sleep
always tends to lean
back and forth.
And my pictures in their frames on the wall
roll and creak
and outside a cold wind blows
through the trees.

And on my way to the car in the morning
the wind blows in one ear and out the other
and freezes my brain.

And it doesn't change a thing, because the ground
still spins under my feet.
And technically it always does, but I feel it
more than most.

Maybe I drink too much coffee,
maybe I listen to my music too loud,
or maybe I have too many thoughts
balled up on one side of my brain,
throwing me off balance.
I try to let them go, but when I do,
the spinning becomes unbearable and
I quickly grab onto whatever's closest.

People, pillows, steering wheels, and keys,
anchor me down,
and we go round and round.

Imperfect

The road out of my neighborhood is
cracked and bumpy.
And it rattles my car, and
the locks don't work in my doors
anymore, and the seats are stained with coffee.
And my voice skitters over music
from the speakers,
and my voice is always slightly out of tune.
Driving home in the evening, the sun
is never out of my eyes, and I'm always
late by five minutes, wherever I go.
Sometimes my girlfriend and I have fights
sometimes we don't fit on
the couch just right.
But we lie there anyway.
Even if the blanket's too small
or the window lets in too much light
we lie there anyway
and somehow, it's right.

Love

I can't stand sappy love poems,
because nobody loves like that.
But I can think of lots of words to describe love.
Love is like when you squint your eyes
and all the images around you turn to shapes,
and the colors mix to form a new picture.
And it's always around you, but it changes
depending on where you are,
how you're feeling,
or who you're with.
Love is a god.
And it funnels through everything and fuels life,
allowing it to go on.
And love is an answer to all the world's problems
and love is all the world's problems.
So when I say that I love you, I mean that
I love you like sand in my shoe, or unpaid insurance
that's due.
I love you like a scratch on my skin, or a screaming,
yelling, kid.
And love can make us feel angry, or unkind,
but without it, we wouldn't be alive.

Old Man and a Dog, Gone

An old man and his dog used to walk by
my house. They both had white hair,
they both took care of each other.
And I don't know if either had a wife,
but I do know the man and his dog were
happy, always. And I could never see a way
where either would be upset, or without the other.
When I pet the dog, I could feel her frailty, and I
could feel years slipping away from her, but even
at a young age, I couldn't picture a world where the
old man would be without the dog. But it goes that
way, doesn't it?
First it's a friend, then it's a partner, then a
grandparent, parent, then spouse. It's your weekly
allowance, your first kiss, first car, first house.
Then it's your dog.

I saw the old man walking alone.

It will be him, someday.

Car Wash Poem #3

In the sweet fragrance of glass cleaner, a
boy and girl look at each other through
the window of a garage door. As rain
begins to fall on the top of the girl's head,
she breathes a cloud onto the glass between
them. The boy blows his own smoke onto
the panel of glass and composes with his
finger tips, a smiling face. The girl draws
around the face, a heart, and they share a
comforting smile as the boy looks at her with
loving eyes. They know they may not be together
forever, but from now and until the next time
he blinks, they will be, and that's enough to
make them smile for the rest of that time.

Between Twilight

A thickly coated on
layer of fog
covers the childhood town where I grew.
A saxophone drives me home
through the familiar streets I knew.

On my way home.

All day, I've wanted nothing more
than to rest my head.
A girl's shoulder is nice,
but it's not my bed,
so I'm on my way home.

I run a stop sign,
stop at the red light
and take the next right.
I don't quite remember the drive, but
I'm home.
Up the stairs, into bed
and I'm home -
in my head.

And time is time until it isn't
perceived and then it's just

space.

And the space between opening and closing my
eyes leaves just that: space.

And there's a place for you,
so I hope that you'll join me there.
If not tonight, next time.
Somewhere in between twilight,
a nightlight,

and my mind.

www.ingramcontent.com/pod-product-compliance
Lightning Source LLC
Chambersburg PA
CBHW031515150726
47990CB00007B/3028